Thatcher Bay, Washington, Nearshore Restoration Assessment

Joel Breems[1]*, Sandy Wyllie-Echeverria[1], Eric Grossman[2], and Joel Elliott[3]

Open-File Report 2008-1369

Prepared for:

Skagit Fisheries Enhancement Group
407 Main Street, Suite 212
Mount Vernon, WA 98273

SKAGIT FISHERIES
ENHANCEMENT GROUP

[1]University of Washington, Friday Harbor Labs and UW Botanic Gardens, Box 354115, Seattle,WA
      98195.
[2]U.S. Geological Survey, Pacific Science Center, 400 Natural Bridges Dr., Santa Cruz, CA 95060.
[3]University of Puget Sound, Department of Biology, 1500 N. Warner, Tacoma, WA 98416.
*Corresponding author, jbreems@u.washington.edu.

U.S. Department of the Interior
KEN SALAZAR, Secretary

U.S. Geological Survey
Suzette M. Kimball, Acting Director

U.S. Geological Survey, Reston, Virginia 2009

For product and ordering information:
World Wide Web: http://www.usgs.gov/pubprod
Telephone: 1-888-ASK-USGS

For more information on the USGS—the Federal source for science about the Earth,
its natural and living resources, natural hazards, and the environment:
World Wide Web: http://www.usgs.gov
Telephone: 1-888-ASK-USGS

Contents

List of Figures

List of Tables

Appendices

Conversion Factors

Inch/Pound to SI

Multiply	By	To obtain
Length		
inch (in.)	2.54	centimeter (cm)
inch (in.)	25.4	millimeter (mm)
foot (ft)	0.3048	meter (m)
Area		
acre	4,047	square meter (m^2)
acre	0.4047	hectare (ha)
acre	0.4047	square hectometer (hm^2)
acre	0.004047	square kilometer (km^2)

Temperature in degrees Celsius (°C) may be converted to degrees Fahrenheit (°F) as follows:
°F=(1.8×°C)+32

Temperature in degrees Fahrenheit (°F) may be converted to degrees Celsius (°C) as follows:
°C=(°F-32)/1.8

Vertical coordinate information is referenced to the insert datum name (and abbreviation) here for instance, "North American Vertical Datum of 1988 (NAVD 88)."

Horizontal coordinate information is referenced to the insert datum name (and abbreviation) here for instance, "North American Datum of 1983 (NAD 83)."

Altitude, as used in this report, refers to distance above the vertical datum.

*Transmissivity: The standard unit for transmissivity is cubic foot per day per square foot times foot of aquifer thickness [(ft^3/d)/ft^2]ft. In this report, the mathematically reduced form, foot squared per day (ft^2/d), is used for convenience.

SI to Inch/Pound

Multiply	By	To obtain
Length		
centimeter (cm)	0.3937	inch (in.)
millimeter (mm)	0.03937	inch (in.)
meter (m)	3.281	foot (ft)
Area		
square meter (m²)	0.0002471	acre
hectare (ha)	2.471	acre
square hectometer (hm²)	2.471	acre
square kilometer (km²)	247.1	acre
hectare (ha)	0.003861	square mile (mi²)

Temperature in degrees Celsius (°C) may be converted to degrees Fahrenheit (°F) as follows: °F=(1.8×°C)+32

Temperature in degrees Fahrenheit (°F) may be converted to degrees Celsius (°C) as follows: °C=(°F-32)/1.8

Vertical coordinate information is referenced to the insert datum name (and abbreviation) here, for instance, "North American Vertical Datum of 1988 (NAVD 88)"

Horizontal coordinate information is referenced to the insert datum name (and abbreviation) here, for instance, "North American Datum of 1983 (NAD 83)"

Acknowledgments

This project was funded in part by a grant from the Salmon Recovery Funding Board (SRFB RCO Project #05-1518N) managed by Skagit Fisheries Enhancement Group. We acknowledge the Friday Harbor Laboratories for logistic and technical support, without which this project would not have been possible. Great thanks are due to the many who volunteered for data collection and editorial comments, with special thanks to Joanna Breems for support and assistance.

Executive Summary

The San Juan Archipelago, located at the confluence of the Puget Sound, the Straits of Juan de Fuca in Washington State, and the Straits of Georgia, British Columbia, Canada, provides essential nearshore habitat for diverse salmonid, forage fish, and bird populations. With 408 miles of coastline, the San Juan Islands provide a significant portion of the available nearshore habitat for the greater Puget Sound and are an essential part of the regional efforts to restore Puget Sound (Puget Sound Shared Strategy 2005). The nearshore areas of the San Juan Islands provide a critical link between the terrestrial and marine environments. For this reason the focus on restoration and conservation of nearshore habitat in the San Juan Islands is of paramount importance.

Wood-waste was a common by-product of historical lumber-milling operations. To date, relatively little attention has been given to the impact of historical lumber-milling operations in the San Juan Archipelago. Thatcher Bay, on Blakely Island, located near the east edge of the archipelago, is presented here as a case study on the restoration potential for a wood-waste contaminated nearshore area. Case study components include (1) a brief discussion of the history of milling operations. (2) an estimate of the location and amount of the current distribution of wood-waste at the site, (3) a preliminary examination of the impacts of wood-waste on benthic flora and fauna at the site, and (4) the presentation of several restoration alternatives for the site.

The history of milling activity in Thatcher Bay began in 1879 with the construction of a mill in the southeastern part of the bay. Milling activity continued for more than 60 years, until the mill closed in 1942. Currently, the primary evidence of the historical milling operations is the presence of approximately 5,000 yd^3 of wood-waste contaminated sediments. The distribution and thickness of residual wood-waste at the site was determined by using sediment coring and GIS-based interpolation techniques. Additionally, pilot studies were conducted to characterize in place sediment redox, organic composition, and sulfide impacts to nearshore flora and fauna.

We found that the presence of wood-waste in Thatcher Bay may alter the quality of the benthic habitat by contributing to elevated levels of total organic composition (TOC) of the sediment. Increased TOC favors anaerobic respiration in marine sediments, and sulfide, a toxic by-product of this process, was found at levels as high as 17.5 mg L^{-1} in Thatcher Bay. The Thatcher Bay sulfide levels are several orders of magnitude higher than those known to impact benthic invertebrates.

Eelgrass, *Zostera marina*, located on the western margin of Thatcher Bay, was surveyed by using underwater video surveys. This baseline distribution will in part be used to measure the impact of any future remediation efforts. Additionally, the distribution and survey data can provide an estimate of propagule source for future colonization of restored sediment.

Three restoration alternatives were considered, and a ranking matrix was developed to score each alternative against site-specific and regional criteria. The process identified the removal of wood-waste from a water-based platform as the preferred alternative.

Our multidisciplinary investigation identified the location, thickness, and potential impacts of wood-waste that has persisted in the nearshore environment of Thatcher Bay since at least 1942. We also provide a process to efficiently evaluate alternatives to remediate the impact of this historical disturbance and to potentially contribute to an increase of nearshore diversity and productivity at this site. Elements of this approach could inform restoration planning at similarly impacted sites throughout the region.

Introduction

In recent decades there has been an ongoing change in the public's perception of the importance of functions provided by the environment. In the Pacific Northwest, this change in perception is evidenced by efforts to restore the greater Puget Sound area (Shared Strategy Development Committee 2007). The nearshore environment is an integral link between terrestrial and marine systems and it provides highly productive habitat for many species (Redman and others, 2005). The San Juan Islands has approximately 408 miles of shoreline habitat (Puget Sound Shared Strategy, 2005). Thatcher Bay is located on Blakely Island and is part of the San Juan Archipelago (N48°33.124 W122°48.951; (Figure 1). The San Juan Islands nearshore environments have been identified as a focal area by Skagit Fisheries Enhancement Group (SFEG; Project Restoration Committee, 2004) as well as a restoration priority by Puget Sound Salmon Recovery Plan (Shared Strategy Development Committee, 2007).

Thatcher Bay has a southwestern exposure, and encompasses approximately 21 hectares. The surrounding land is currently held by the Blakely Island Trust. A conservation easement through the San Juan Preservation Trust encompasses all of the backshore[4] and upland areas surrounding Thatcher Bay.

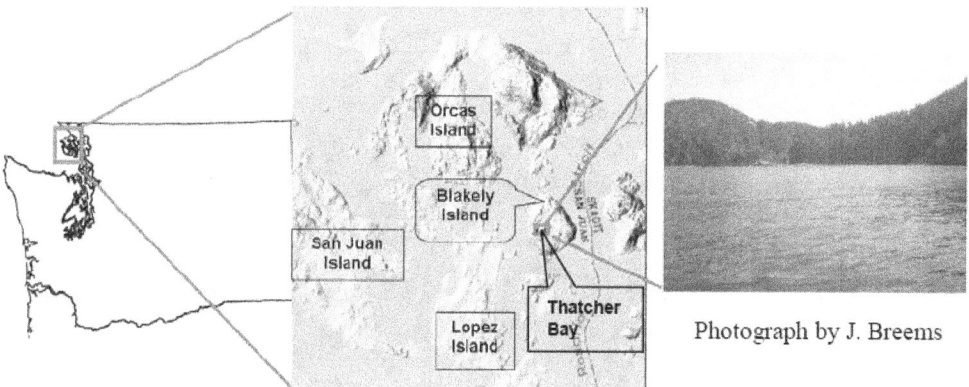

Figure 1. Map of Thatcher Bay, Blakely Island, Washington and surrounding islands along with photograph of the mouth of Thatcher Bay looking east.

The backshore and upland forests of Thatcher Bay are undeveloped. To the passing boater, it appears to contain high quality nearshore[5] habitat, but further examination reveals the degraded nature of this habitat. The nearshore and intertidal sediment contains extensive amounts of wood-waste as a result of historical land uses.

The San Juan Archipelago provides a diversity of nearshore habitats that are needed to support healthy forage fish stocks and provide refuge to migrating and resident populations of juvenile and adult salmon species (Redman and others, 2005; Shared Strategy Development Committee 2007). As a result, restoration of contaminated nearshore habitat has been identified as a priority for salmon recovery by the San Juan County Salmon Recovery Plan.

---

[4] The backshore area is immediately beyond the uppermost limit of the intertidal zone only inundated during extreme tides or storm events (Mayhew, 2008).

[5] The nearshore area includes the intertidal and subtidal zones; it is bounded on the outer margin by the depth to which light can penetrate to the seafloor.

By using the findings of the San Juan County Salmon Recovery Plan as a framework, the objectives of this case study report are: (1) a brief discussion of the history of the site and milling operations (section 2), (2) an estimate of the location and amount of the current distribution of wood-waste at the site (section 3), (3) a preliminary examination of the impacts of wood-waste on benthic flora and fauna at the site (sections 4 and 5), and (4) the presentation of several restoration alternatives for the site (section 7). This report serves as a partial fulfillment of Thatcher Bay Nearshore Assessment and Design Project funded by the Salmon Recovery Funding Board (SRFB RCO Project #05-1518N) and sponsored by SFEG.

History of the Site

Blakely Island is located within the historical territory of the Samish Indian Nation. Blakely Island and Thatcher Bay were used by the Samish people for various purposes, including elk and deer hunting and fishing. There is evidence that the Samish Nation maintained a temporary or seasonal camp in Thatcher Bay (Suttles, 1951). It does not appear that there were any permanent settlements on the island until the arrival of Euro-American settlers in the late 1800s (Hayner, 1929).

The exact dates of the first settlement of Blakely Island are unclear; however, it is known that by 1879, William Harrison Coffelt and his brothers had established the town of Thatcher, Washington, and constructed a sawmill (Roe, 2005). The original mill used a reciprocating saw powered by water from Spencer Lake (Figure 2). Later the facility was upgraded to steam power and a more efficient circular saw.

Figure 2. Aerial photograph showing the location of the Spencer Mill in relation to Spencer Creek and Lake.

The sawmill operation was sold to Theodore Spencer and renamed Spencer Mill Company in 1892 (Figure 3). The mill's main products were lumber, fruit, and fish boxes, and later included seine boat manufacturing. During its peak operation, Spencer Mill was known as one of the largest mills north of Seattle (Roe, 2005). The Spencer

Mill processed timber from surrounding islands in the San Juan Archipelago, as well as from Blakely Island. This timber processing activity, along with the associated logging, supported the town of Thatcher, Washington. According to an 1897 census, Blakely Island had a population of 56. The population increased to 86 by 1910, only to decline to 25 by 1920 (Hayner, 1929). This population decline coincided with the slowing of logging operations on the island, which ceased in 1929 (Roe, 2005). Activity at the Spencer Mill began to decrease by the mid 1930s and the mill closed in 1942.

After the closing of the mill, its legacy persisted with the abandoned buildings, and the area was known as "sawdust beach" by the local residents (Roe, 2005). The failure of the Spencer Lake dam in 1965 resulted in a blowout that removed most evidence of the mill structures. The wood-waste present in the nearshore remains the primary evidence of past operations.

Figure 3. Historical photographs or the Spencer Mill house, town of Thatcher, Washington, and the mill house and dock loaded with milled timber taken soon after 1892. Courtesy of Buck and Shirley Plummer.

Sources of Wood-waste

There is no evidence of timber production or wood manipulation activities by the Samish Indian Nation or other tribes in the region that could have contributed to the current accumulation of wood-waste. Thatcher Bay experiences heavy storms in the winter months, and has a relatively large fetch[6] to the southwest that allows for accumulation of drift wood and wrack during these seasonal storm events (Hubbert, L.,

[6] A fetch is an area of ocean or lake surface over which the wind blows in an essentially constant direction, thus generating waves (Encyclopedia Britannica, 2008).

personal commun., 2007). The typical drift wood is not consistent with the fine wood-waste found within Thatcher Bay and is not thought to contribute in any significant manner to the wood-waste load within the Bay. Current logging activities on Blakely Island are limited to occasional stand-thinning harvests and use of a log dump in the northeast corner of the Bay. There has been no logging activity or use of the log dump since 2006, and there are no plans to resume operations (Hubbert, L., written commun., 2008).

Log dumping and booming operations consist of placing cut timber into the bay by using a metal rack designed to protect the shore. The logs are then secured within a boom for future transport by tugboat. During this process there is frequent collision and abrasion between the logs, scouring off bark or coarse woody debris. SCUBA surveys, conducted as a permitting requirement for log dumping and booming operations in the northeastern section of Thatcher Bay in 1993, 1994, and 1997, reveal little woody debris associated with logging activities. (Pentec Environmental Inc., 1994; Pentec Environmental Inc., 1997). The woody debris, produced as a result of dumping and booming operations, typically consists of bark and coarse woody debris; in contrast, the wood-waste in the southeastern corner of Thatcher Bay is primarily of a very fine consistency.

Evidence points to the Spencer Mill as the primary source of the current wood-waste deposited in the southeastern corner of Thatcher Bay. It is unclear if the by-products of milling (for example, wood-waste and bark) were deposited directly into the adjacent nearshore areas, or were moved to this location at a later time. The Spencer Mill likely reached peak capacity between 1887 and 1930 (Hayner, 1929; Roe, 2005). It is probable that the majority of the wood-waste production would have coincided with this peak in milling operations.

Wood-waste Over Time

By using available historical and current evidence, combined with field observations and sampling, we conclude that the wood-waste from Spencer Mill has persisted in the intertidal region since at least the 1930s. While there is no documentation on the movement of wood-waste deposited in Thatcher Bay, there is anecdotal evidence from the residents of Blakely Island that the amount of wood-waste exposed at low tide has diminished over time; however, this has not been verified.

Given the water current and drift-cell patterns within Thatcher Bay, transportation of the wood-waste off site is unlikely (Figure 4). Drift cells are erosion and depositional patterns influenced by tidal movement, prevailing winds, and geography of the region (Shoreland and Environmental Assistance Program, 2002). The convergence of the prevailing drift-cells near the project site would result in minimal transportation of wood-waste from the impacted area. It is more likely that persistent wave and tidal action has caused settling of the wood-waste in the sediment matrix. This theory is supported by the coring done in August 2007 as part of this project; findings are discussed in the Assessment of Wood-waste Distribution and Abundance section.

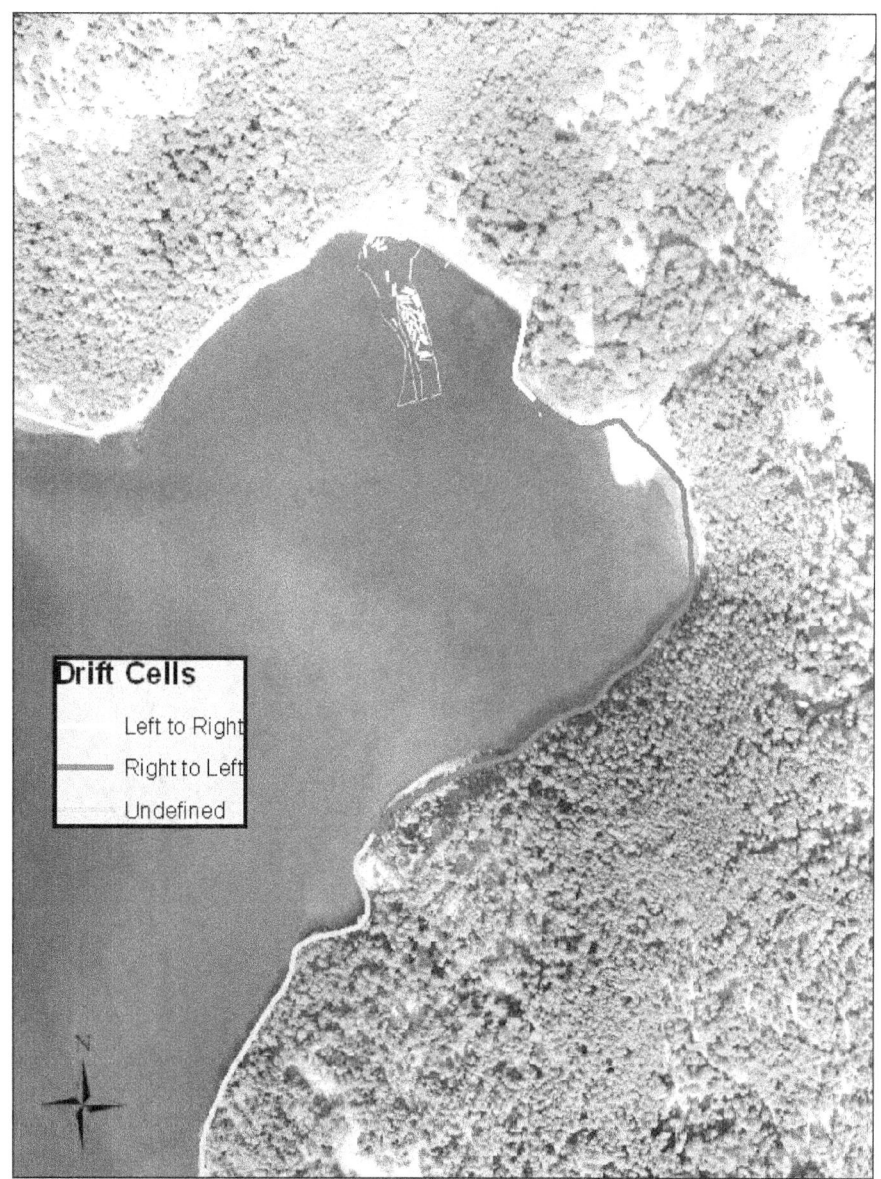

Figure 4. Annotated color infrared photograph showing prevailing drift-cell patterns in Thatcher Bay, Washington.

There are several series of aerial photographs of the Thatcher Bay area from 1965 to present (Figure 5) courtesy of the Washington Coastal Atlas (http://www.ecy.wa.gov/programs/sea/sma/atlas_home.html). While it is not possible to determine the movement of the wood-waste over time by using these photos, the signature of the wood-waste remains visible. The failure of the Spencer Lake dam in 1965 caused significant movement of upland rocky sediments into the nearshore. The persistence of this rocky substrate and wood-waste are visible in the aerial photographs.

Figure 5. Photographs showing the persistence of wood-waste (red arrows) in Thatcher Bay since 1965.

Assessment of Wood-waste Distribution and Abundance

Coring Assessment

Historical records reveal that milling operations were likely the primary source of wood-waste in Thatcher Bay. In order to determine which nearshore habitat types and functions have been degraded, an accurate delineation of the impacted area is necessary. Our objective was to determine the vertical and horizontal distribution of wood-waste at the site in order to estimate the volume of impacted sediments. This is essential in order to provide guidance to the development of appropriate remediation alternatives.

Methods

On August 23, 2007, sediment cores were obtained by using a split-core auger system. Thirty-two sediment cores were taken every fifty ft. along six predefined transects perpendicular to shore (Figure 6). Several pilot cores, outside the six predefined transects, were included in the analysis of wood-waste distribution. All cores were measured, and segments were assigned to one of five categories: surface sediment, wood, sediment/wood, dense sediment wood and basal sediment. Precautions were taken to ensure that the core remained intact for measurement purposes. Due to the compaction of the wood-waste and sediment inherent to the coring process, some cores may underestimate the amount of wood-waste within individual sampling locations. An estimate of compaction levels for each core appears in Appendix A.

6

Figure 6. Location of the sediment cores in Thatcher Bay, Washington.

Figure 7 shows the process of measuring the core. Surface sediment (A) was defined as any sediment located above wood-waste. Wood (B) was used to define any portion of the core where the composition was found to be mostly wood-waste. Sediment/wood and dense sediment wood (C) were two categories used to describe any portion of the core where sediment and wood-waste were visibly intermixed. Dense sediment wood was used to describe core segments where wood-waste composed less than 20 percent of the sediment. Basal sediment (D) was all sediment found below the last visible wood-waste in the core. All cores were labeled and photographed at high resolution for future reference. If the basal sediments were not reached, a second core was taken to determine the maximum depth of wood-waste deposition.

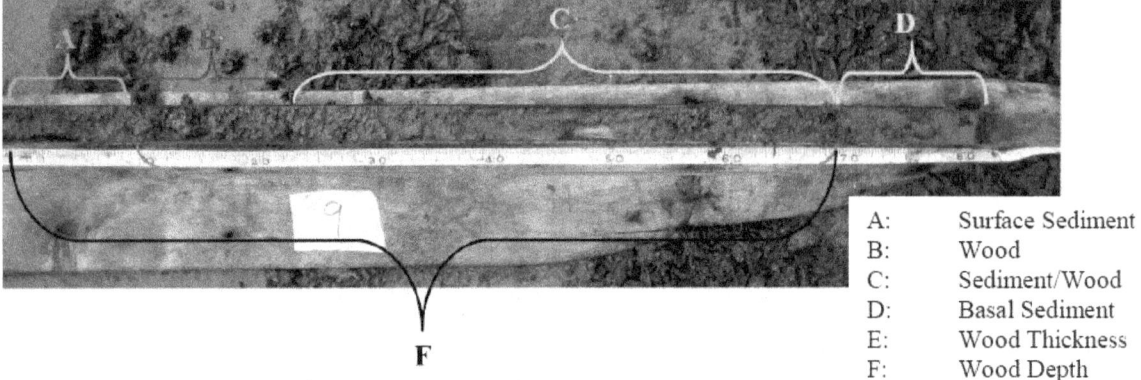

A:	Surface Sediment
B:	Wood
C:	Sediment/Wood
D:	Basal Sediment
E:	Wood Thickness
F:	Wood Depth

Figure 7. Photograph showing visual representation of sediment categories, taken fro Thatcher Bay, Washington. See text for explanation.

Maximum wood depth and thickness were calculated for all cores as shown in Figure 7. Maximum depth (F) was calculated by combining the surface sediment, wood, sediment/wood, and dense sediment wood categories. The result is the maximum depth, in meters, that wood-waste was observed. The same method was used to determine wood thickness (E) with the exclusion of the surface sediment category. Locations and details of core measurements are listed in appendix A.

By using data from the core samples, ArcGIS was used to estimate distribution patterns using inverse distance weighting (IDW). The IDW process estimates the value of points between measured values based on distance from the reference points. For both wood thickness and depth, the parameters for the IDW tool were set to use the weighted averages of twelve reference points. The total volume of contaminated sediment was determined by averaging the maximum wood depth for all the cores and multiplying it by the total area of the site as follows:

Volume = Area (m^2) * $(\sum depth/n)$.

Results and Discussion

Figures 8 and 9 display the spatial interpolation of the data obtained from core samples (see appendix A). Figure 8 illustrates a concentration of wood-waste in the center of the project site at approximately 1-2 ft below Mean Lower Low Water (MLLW). This concentration of wood-waste corresponds with cores 6 and 8. By using landmarks in the historical photos of the Spencer Mill (Figure 3), it can be estimated that cores 6 and 8 correspond with the historical location of the mill, the concentration of wood-waste shown in Figure 9 supports this observation, as well. The distribution determined by the IDW analysis indicates that there is a trend of reduced wood-waste thickness and depth with distance from the shore and site of the mill. Assuming a conservative 0.55 m (1.8 ft) for average depth of the wood-waste and contaminated sediments, there are approximately 3,792 m^3 of wood-waste and wood-waste contaminated sediments in the impacted area.

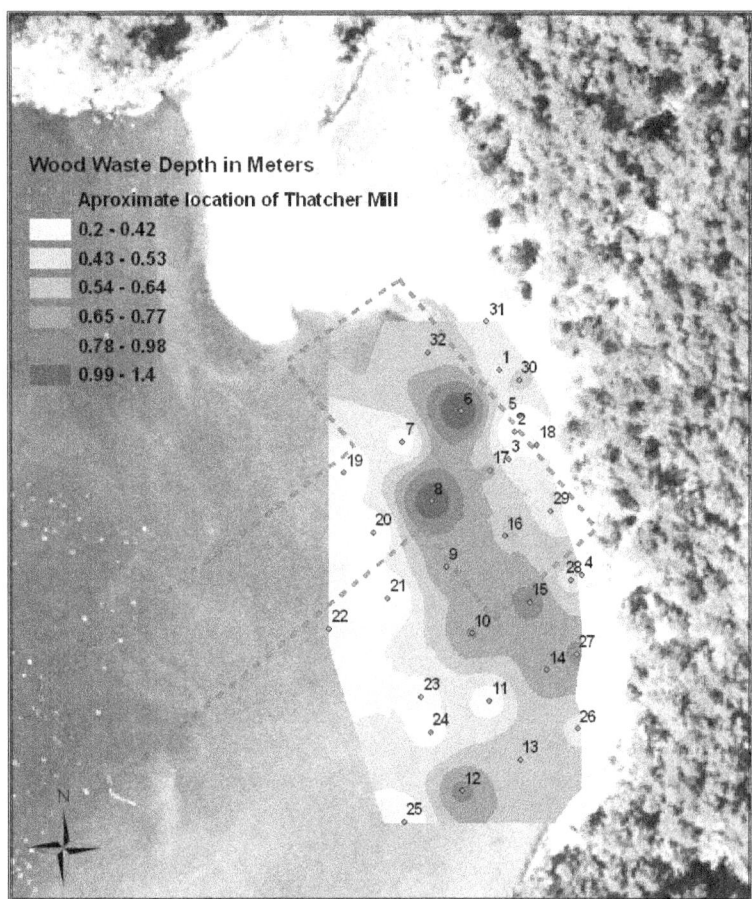

Figure 8. Map of the maximum depth of wood-waste observed in Thatcher Bay and approximate extent of historic mill house (red dashed line). Color is indicative of depth below the sediment surface. Darker colors indicate deeper depths. A general trend of decreasing depth along transects perpendicular to shore was observed.

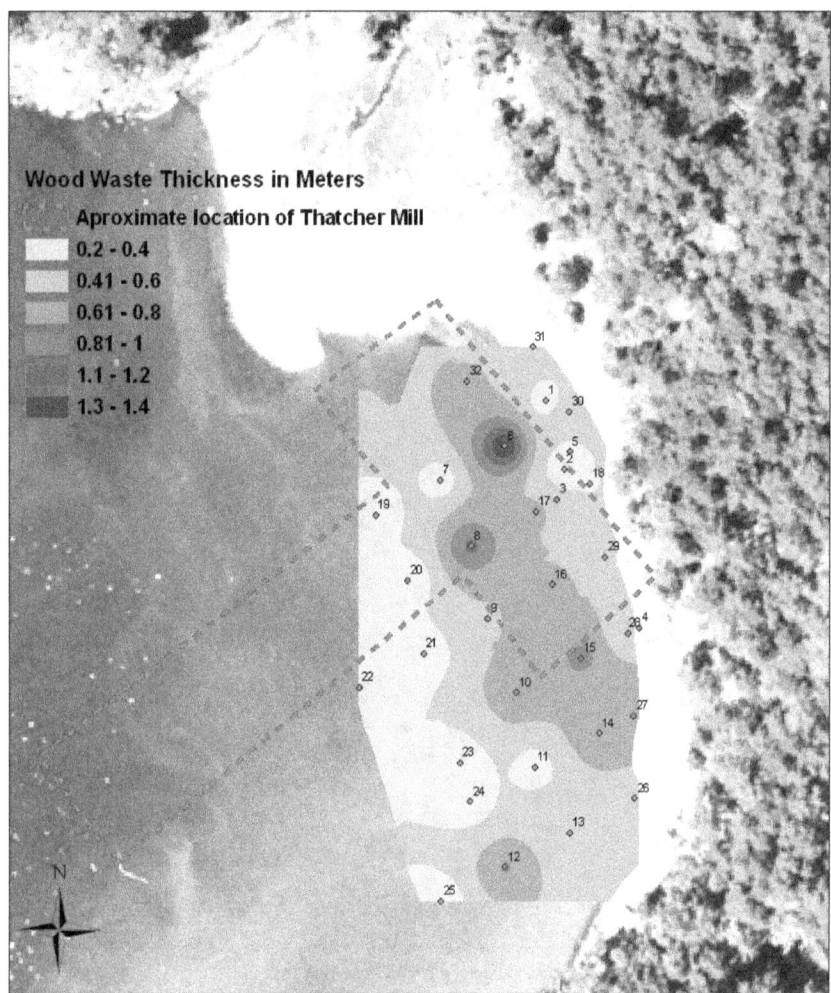

Figure 9. Map of the maximum thickness of wood-waste observed in Thatcher Bay and approximate extent of historic mill house (red dashed line). Color gradient represents thickness of wood-waste deposit. Wood thickness distribution is strongly correlated to wood depth.

Impacts to Benthic Flora and Fauna

Redox Potential and Sulfide Levels

Oxygen is depleted rapidly in marine sediments, usually within the first few millimeters of the sediment surface (Holmer and others, 2005; Philips, 1984). In order to breakdown organic material in an anoxic environment, alternative electron acceptors must be used (for example, sulfate). Some of the by-products of this process are the production of sulfide and more reduced sediments (Gayaldo, 2002; Hyland and others, 2005). Sulfide can be toxic to marine flora and fauna (Wang and Chapman, 1999) and has been shown to reduce benthic invertebrate species diversity and abundance (Hyland and others, 2005). Increased organic material in the sediment facilitates elevated anaerobic respiration and the production of sulfide. Fine wood-waste, such as that found in Thatcher Bay, greatly increases the organic composition of the sediments. Our objective was to compare the redox potential and sulfide levels elevated in the wood-waste contaminated areas of Thatcher Bay with Picnic Cove (N48°33.940 W 122° 55.459; (Fig. 10) to determine if there is an impact to the benthic flora and faunal communities of Thatcher Bay. Picnic Cove was chosen as a reference site because *Zostera marina* has been monitored annually in the area through the Submerged Vegetation Monitoring Project (Gaeckle, 2007) and, although this site faces to the south, it has a protected backshore and shape like those of Thatcher Bay.

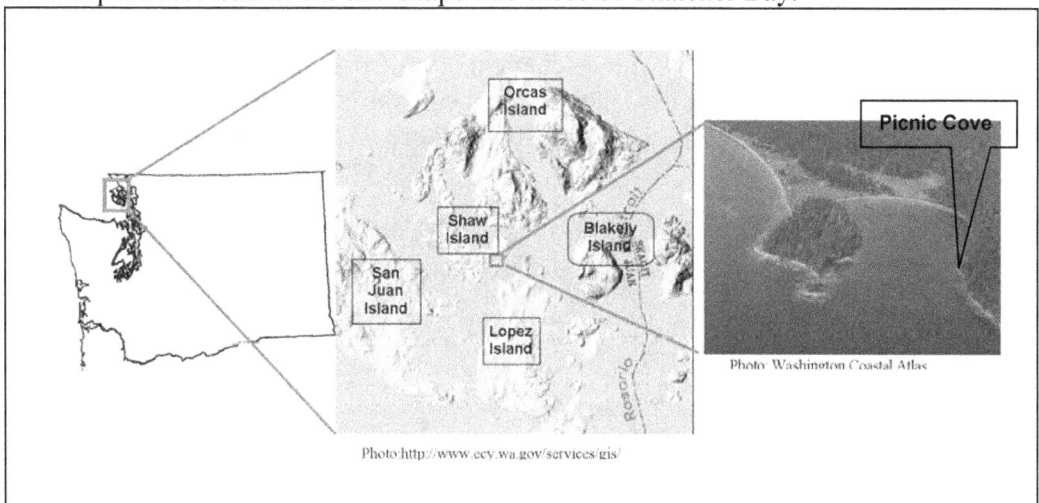

Figure 10. Map showing Picnic Cove located on Shaw Island, Washington. This site served as a reference site for several pilot studies.

Methods

Sediment cores were collected from Thatcher Bay and Picnic Cove for use in a mesocosm growth experiment (See Mesocosm Growth Data section) as well as for analysis of redox potential. Of the ten cores collected from Picnic cove, five contained *Zostera marina* (eelgrass) ramets[7] (PC) and five did not (PCS). The remaining five cores were collected from Thatcher Bay (TB), without *Z. marina,* for a

---

[7] In the case of *Z. marina,* a complete ramet consists of rhizome, roots, and a vegetative shoot.

11

total of fifteen cores. All cores were collected with a 15 cm diameter corer and were taken from approximately 1 ft below MLLW.

Sediment cores were analyzed at Friday Harbor Labs. Redox measurements were made at a depth of 1.5-2 cm for all cores containing only sediment (TB, PCS). The measurements were collected by using an ORP-146C (Lazar Research Labs) combination probe and a 6230 microcomputer (Jenco) and results were expressed in Mv.

An additional 15 cm diameter core was collected, for redox analysis (TBR), from the same location as the sediment cores in Thatcher Bay, by using a 3 inch diameter PVC tube. The TBR core was taken below the water line and capped with no head space. Redox measurements for the TBR core were taken every 2 cm along the vertical axis in a closed nitrogen environment to prevent sulfide oxidation. The sulfide levels were determined by using the Colorimetric Method as described in USEPA Methods for Chemical Analysis of Water and Wastes, Method 376.2 (1983) and APHA Standard Methods, 20th ed, p. 4-165, method 4500-S2- D (1998) (Chemetrics, 2008). Pore-water was collected by centrifuging sediment and extracting the pore water. All processing was conducted in a nitrogen environment to preserve the samples. Sulfide levels were tested by using Chemetrics' test kits, which measure total acid-soluble sulfides and employ methylene blue methodology (Chemetrics, 2008). Results are expressed as ppm and are converted to mg L^{-1}.

Results and Discussion

The redox potentials for the sediment cores (TB and PCS) and the TBR core are displayed in tables 1 and 2. All of the sediment cores from Thatcher Bay (TB and TBR) were more highly reducing than the sediment cores from Picnic Cove (PCS). Pore-water sulfide levels derived from the TBR core were 17.5 mg L^{-1} in the first 6 cm (table 3).

Table 1. Sediment core Redox potential (Mv) of Thatcher Bay (TB) and Picnic Cove (PCS), Washington.

Site	Redox, in Mv	Site	Redox, in Mv
TB 1	-146	PCS 1	-66
TB 2	-160	PCS 2	-41
TB 3	-110	PCS 3	-114
TB 4	-161	PCS 4	-62
TB 5	-114	PCS 5	-111

Table 2. The redox potential measurements for the Thatcher Bay Redox core were taken along the vertical axis with measurements concentrated at the upper end of the core to resolve the impact of surface sediment/water interactions.

Depth	Redox
0.5	-234
1	-181
1.75	-235
2.25	-232
3	-237
3.75	-235
4.75	-239
5.75	-233
6.5	-215
7	-231
7.5	-233
8	-237
9	-231
10	-232
11	-234
12	-218
13	-219
14	-225
15	-217

Table 3. Sulfide levels derived from the pore water from the Thatcher Bay Redox core. Sulfide levels as low as .02 mg L^{-1} can begin to impact the invertebrate community through decreased productivity and increased mortality (Hyland and others, 2005).

Depth, in cm	Sulfide level, in mg L^{-1}
0-2	17.5
2-4	17.5
4-6	17.5
6-8	16.0
8-10	15.0
10-12	6.0

Both redox potential and sulfide levels were elevated, potentially as a result of increased organic composition of the sediment. As sulfide levels increase there is the potential for significant alteration of the nearshore benthic community. Wang and Chapman (1999) outlined toxicity levels for various species in the benthic environment (appendix B). There is a broad range of sulfide levels that are considered toxic, 1 mg L^{-1} to >50 mg L^{-1}; however, a number of species experience toxicity below these levels (Wang and Chapman, 1999). The sulfide levels of 17.5 mg L^{-1} found in Thatcher Bay would be highly toxic to many species. The expected impact is decreased diversity and density of the invertebrate community favoring those more highly adapted to anoxic conditions.

The discrepancy in redox potentials between tables 1 and 2 is likely a result of a variation in the collection protocol. The sediment cores collected for the purpose of the mesocosm growth experiment were exposed to ambient air during collection and transport. This exposure could alter the redox potential of the sediment. The TBR core was not exposed to ambient air and was processed in a nitrogen environment, allowing for a more accurate measure of redox

Sediment cores collected in Thatcher Bay were analyzed for redox and sulfide levels as part of a pilot study. The results begin to reveal the nature of the sediment chemistry in Thatcher Bay and serve as an indicator that redox and sulfide levels could be elevated across Thatcher Bay.

Total Organic Composition

Elevated organic composition of the sediment can create conditions favorable to anaerobic respiration leading to increased sulfide levels (Hyland and others, 2005). Many areas in the southeastern corner of Thatcher Bay have high concentrations of wood-waste, which in turn increases organic composition of the sediments. There is no established percentage composition of organic material that is considered harmful, however above 5 percent is generally considered elevated (Koch 2001). Healthy *Zostera marina* (eelgrass) beds, which are highly productive and provide spawning for Pacific Herring, and refuge for outmigrating juvenile salmon (Philips, 1984), have been documented as having a range of organic composition from 1.25 percent to 16 percent (of dry weight; Koch, 2001).

A high percentage of organic matter in the sediment can lead to increased sulfide production through anaerobic respiration; in order to survive, *Z. marina* would require a high availability of light, efficient photosynthesis, and ideal water quality (Holmer and others, 2005; Koch, 2001; Goodman and others, 1995). Our objective was to determine if the organic composition of Thatcher Bay sediment was elevated.

Methods

Sediment for use in this analysis was subsampled from the same sediment collected for use in the sulfide analysis in the Redox Potential and Sulfide Levels section from Thatcher Bay (TB) and Picnic Cove (PCS). Percent organic composition was determined by using the loss on ignition method (LOI) as described by the Soil Society of America (Nelson and Sommers, 1994). All sediment samples were air dried for 48 hours prior to grinding and sieving them through a 500 μM screen to ensure homogenization and complete combustion. Sediment was then placed in pre weighed crucibles, dried at 105°C for 24 hours, weighed, and fired at 400°C for 12 hours. Following the firing process, the samples were weighed to determine loss on ignition, and the percent organic composition was calculated. The percent organic composition was then averaged for the samples from each site.

Results and Discussion

Thatcher Bay sediments returned an average organic composition of >6 percent (fig. 11). Picnic Cove, which supports a *Z. marina* population, returned an average organic composition of <1 percent, well below the levels found in Thatcher Bay. The elevated organic composition of the Thatcher Bay sediments informs our understanding of the ongoing impacts of wood-waste within Thatcher Bay.

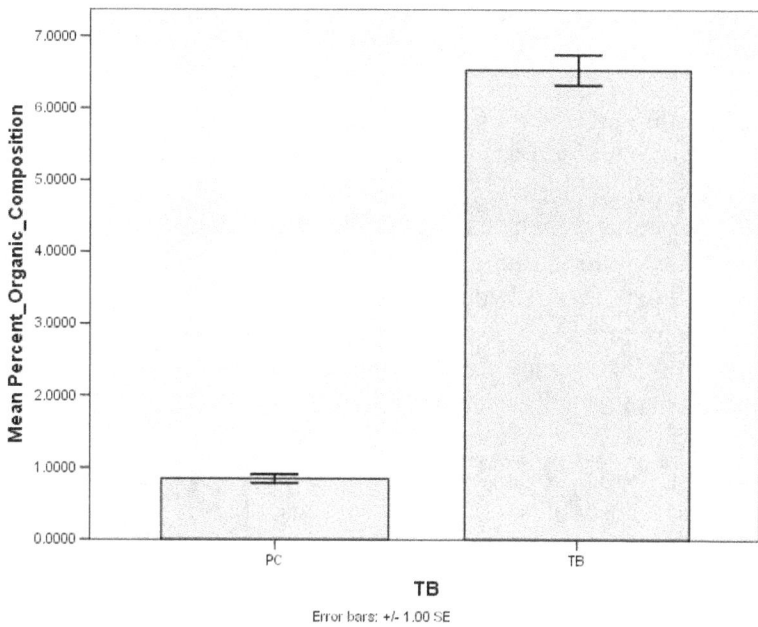

Figure 11. Plot of average percent organic matter (and +/- 1 SE) in Thatcher Bay (TB) and Picnic Cove (PC) sediments determined by using loss on ignition.

The accuracy of LOI method to determine percent-organic composition may be limited in this situation due to the coarse grain of the wood-waste being partially filtered out by the sieve prior to ignition. The result would be an artificially low LOI and percent-organic composition. The sediment used in this experiment contained surface sediment intermixed with wood-waste. As demonstrated in the Assessment of Wood Waste Distribution and Abundance section, there are large portions of the site where wood-waste dominates the sediment composition. It is expected that organic composition of the sediment would correlate strongly with the wood-waste distribution.

Eelgrass Mapping Within Thatcher Bay

The presence of *Zostera marina* (eelgrass) on the Western margin of Thatcher Bay has been previously documented (Pentec Environmental, Inc., 1994; Pentec Environmental, Inc., 1997); however the full extent of the population and its stability over time were unknown. Our objectives were to determine (1) the baseline boundaries of the existing *Z. marina* population prior to the initiation of potential remediation activities, (2) the spatial relationship between the *Z. marina* population and the presence of wood-waste, and, (3) if the existing *Z. marina* population could serve as a viable donor stock in future restoration efforts.

Methods

Underwater video surveys were conducted by using methods described by Elliott and others, (2006). Underwater video equipment was towed at slow speeds from a small boat. Location data, collected with a Garmin GPS unit, were embedded on the video tape, while depth data was collected with a Furuno depth sounder and time coded and saved by using a Trimble GeoXT. The video images and depth data were analyzed by using MediaMapper to determine the outer margin of the existing *Z. marina* bed. If any shoots were seen to be rooted in the video image, *Z. marina* was considered to be present

(Elliott and others, 2006). The video with embedded GPS coordinates was used to develop a map of *Z. marina* for 2006 and 2007.

Results and Discussion

Maps created from video data collected during 2006 and 2007 are displayed in Figure 12 Figure 13. The data show that the current distribution of *Z. marina* is limited to the mouth of Thatcher Bay. The extant population remained in a relatively similar position during the two years of sampling.

The use of a boat during the data collection prevented the exact replication of transect lines between years. As a result, the different surveys covered slightly different areas of the bay. This discrepancy could create an appearance of greater variability in *Z. marina* across years than actually occurs.

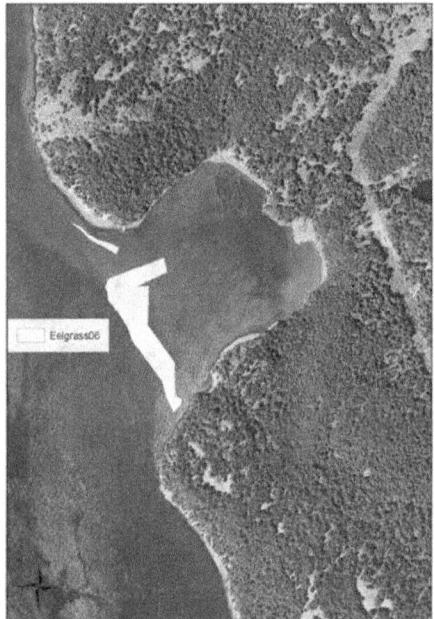

Figure 12. Photograph showing the extent of the eelgrass present in Thatcher Bay, Washington, in 2006.

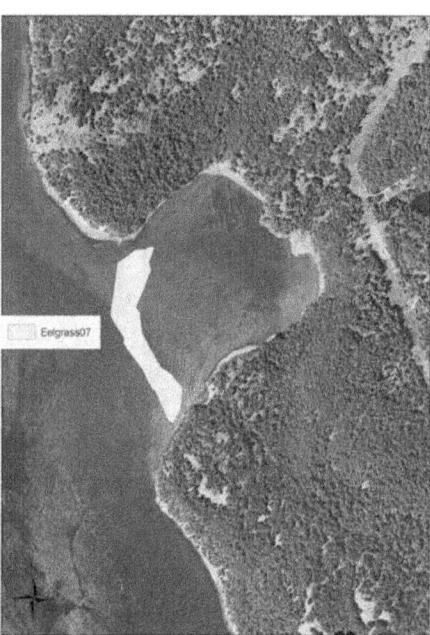

Figure 13. Photograph showing the extent of the eelgrass present in Thatcher Bay, Washington, in 2007.

Mesocosm Growth Data

Z. marina and other seagrass species are directly affected by elevated organic composition and increased sulfide levels (Koch, 2001). Elevated sulfide levels within the sediments and meristimatic tissue of *Z. marina* can lead to a corresponding decrease in photosynthetic efficiency, as well as an increased demand for photosynthetically derived oxygen to maintain oxygen level in the rooting zone (Holmer and others, 2005; Goodman and others, 1995). The oxygenated zone is necessary to oxidize sulfide into sulfate and prevent sulfide intrusion into the plant. As sulfide levels increase, more photosynthetically derived oxygen is required to prevent sulfide intrusion. *Z. marina* is adapted to elevated sulfide environments, but as the levels increase beyond the capacity of the plant to maintain an oxygenated rhizosphere sulfide, intrusion may occur. This intrusion could cause mortality or reduced vigor in the plant (Holmer and others, 2005; Koch, 2001)

The level at which the sulfides are able to penetrate into the rhizome is directly related to the light available (Koch, 2001). As a result, any factor that influences the photosynthetic capacity of *Z. marina* can in turn affect the level at which sulfide is able to penetrate the rhizome. Some of these factors include dissolved oxygen in the water column (Pedersen and others, 2004), light availability (diurnal/seasonal change, algal blooms, and turbidity; Koch, 2001; Zimmerman and others, 1991), epiphyte load (Philips, 1984), and nutrient loading (Koch, 2001; Short and Wyllie-Echeverria, 1996). In order to determine if the current sediment conditions are limiting the distribution of *Z. marina* in the southeastern corner of Thatcher Bay, a mesocosm growth experiment was conducted.

Methods

A seawater mesocosm was used to control light, salinity, temperature, and flow for this growth experiment. The sediment and individual ramets used for this experiment were collected from two locations, Thatcher Bay and Picnic Cove. Sediment plugs were gathered by using a 15 cm diameter PVC pipe with a chiseled edge to aid in sediment penetration. All sediment plugs were placed in 1 gallon plastic pots lined with plastic bags to retain the sediments; care was taken to preserve the sediment profile. Ten sediment plugs and 10 loose ramets (without sediment) were collected randomly from approximately one ft below MLLW from Picnic Cove. Five of these sediment plugs were gathered inside an existing *Z. marina* bed and contained at least one ramet. The remaining five sediment plugs from Picnic Cove were collected from sediment, which was immediately adjacent to the eelgrass (≤1m) and did not contain any ramets. The 10 loose ramets were collected from the same location and stored for later transplant into the blank sediment plugs. The remaining 5 sediment plugs (out of a total of 15) were collected on July 14, 2007, from approximately one ft below MLLW in Thatcher Bay; the cores did not contain *Z. marina* as it is not present in the impacted area.

The 10 loose ramets were transplanted into the 10 sediment cores from Picnic Cove and Thatcher Bay. All 15 sediment cores were randomly arranged in the seawater. Growth was measured by using methods outlined by Short and Duarte (2001); a small hole was made in the leaf sheath by using a probe, allowing the measurement of leaf elongation. Leaf elongation and the initiation of new leaves originate within the leaf sheath. Growth was measured from the static position of the scar on the outer leaves, to the position of the scar on the new leaf tissue. Measured over time, it is possible to establish leaf elongation rates for each ramet. Results were analyzed by using the SPSS (v13.0). An analysis of variance (ANOVA) was performed on leaf elongation rates for all treatments.

Results and Discussion

There was no significant difference in the growth rates between the three treatments with an F value 2.017, degrees of freedom 2, and significance value of 0.137.

This indicates that the sediment alone may not be limiting eelgrass growth within Thatcher Bay. The sediments used for this experiment were from the same location where sulfide, redox, and LOI tests were performed. Redox was measured prior to the mesocosm experiment (section 0), and LOI tests were done following the experiment (Total Organic Composition section). Both pilot studies used the same sediments used in this mesocosm experiment. In both cases the LOI and sulfide levels were sub optimal for *Z. marina* growth (Hyland and others, 2005; Koch, 2001).

Currently no *Z. marina* is present inside the region dominated by wood-waste in Thatcher Bay. The mesocosm growth experiment suggests that *Z. marina* establishment may be possible; however, additional factors could be currently limiting *Z. marina* distribution in Thatcher Bay. In order to survive under the sediments, *Z. marina* requires a highly favorable light environment (Holmer and others, 2005), which was provided for in the mesocosm experiment. The combination of elevated sulfide in the sediments and reduced submarine light could potentially limit *Z. marina* distribution within Thatcher Bay. To investigate if light levels were reduced in Thatcher Bay compared to Picnic Cove, we analyzed light availability by using the pilot studies described below.

Photosynthetically Active Radiation

The elevated percent organic-composition and sulfide levels present in Thatcher Bay could create a higher demand for photosynthetically derived oxygen in *Z. marina*. This could lead to an increased light requirement in degraded sediment sites than in similar sites with more favorable sediment conditions. The light attenuation coefficient (K_d) in which *Z. marina* is known to survive has a range from .16 to1.21 (Dennison and others, 1993). To determine if light availability in Thatcher Bay was limiting *Z. marina* distribution, light was measured in both Picnic Cove and Thatcher Bay.

Methods

Light in the form of photosynthetically active radiation (PAR) was measured weekly in Thatcher Bay and Picnic Cove by using a LiCor LI-193SA spherical sensor, which measures PAR in $\mu mol\ s^{-1}\ m^{-2}$. PAR consists of light with wavelengths between 400 and 700 nm and is the portion of the electromagnetic light spectrum responsible for photosynthesis (Duncan, 1990). Three transects were established in Thatcher Bay and one in Picnic Cove. Transects were sampled during solar noon (1000-1400) at both sites on the same day (Carruthers and others, 2001). The light attenuation coefficient (K_d) of the water column was determined by using methods described by Carruthers and others, (2001).

Results and Discussion

The light attenuation coefficient for both Thatcher Bay and Picnic Cove was 0.288 (R^2 was 0.524 and 0.608 respectively). PAR measurements were taken at both sites on five separate occasions between July 07, 2007 and August 28, 2007.

Dennison and others, (1993) and Zimmerman and others, (1991) document a range of attenuation coefficients in existing *Z. marina* beds between 0.16 and 1.21. The attenuation coefficients of both Thatcher Bay and Picnic Cove are within this range. Picnic Cove currently supports a *Z. marina* population whereas Thatcher Bay does not. The mesocosm growth experiment in the Mecocosm Growth Data section suggested that, given a positive light environment, *Z. marina* could survive in the elevated sulfide levels of the sediment of Thatcher Bay. However, an additional factor which should be considered is the topography of Thatcher Bay. Thatcher Bay is surrounded on all sides by steep slopes that block the southern horizon. This effectively shortens the day length, and reduces the amount of submarine PAR reaching the southern sections of the Bay creating potentially stressful conditions. While submarine PAR in Thatcher Bay is not likely limited during summer months, the combination of decreased light during the winter months and elevated sulfide in the sediment could contribute to a hostile environment for *Z. marina*. As sediment conditions improve, allowing for more effective storage of photosynthetically derived energy, it is possible that the population of *Z. marina*, located at the mouth of Thatcher Bay, could establish new colonies in other areas.

GIS Light Analysis

Field observations over the course of the summer 2007 highlighted several factors unique to Thatcher Bay. The presence of wood-waste in the sediments was determined to increase sulfide levels. The mesocosm experiment suggested that, with a favorable light environment, *Z. marina* could survive with the elevated sulfide levels found in the Thatcher Bay sediments. Given that there are seasonal changes in the light available within Thatcher Bay, light could be limiting *Z. marina* survival during particular seasons of the year. This could be a direct result of the increased light requirements associated with the elevated sulfide levels found in Thatcher Bay.

Methods

By using the area solar radiation tool available in the Spatial Analyst toolbox in ArcMAP 9.2, we modeled the light availability in Thatcher Bay. The solar radiation tool uses an elevation raster and the known position of sun to predict light availability for individual locations on a map. By using the Digital Elevation Model (DEM) for the region, it is possible to predict the amount of solar radiation received by each region of Thatcher Bay. The DEM was used in conjunction with the area solar radiation tool to determine incoming solar radiation in the form of total number of hours of direct sunlight. For the purposes of this report, we chose the number of hours of direct sunlight available for 2007.

Results and Discussion

Figure 14 displays the total hours of direct sunlight received by each region in the bay as a proxy of available atmospheric PAR relative to the distribution of *Z. marina* in 2007 from Figure 13. The darker colors correspond to fewer hours of direct sunlight exposure.

This modeling exercise demonstrates that the topography of Thatcher Bay may have an effect on the light availability of atmospheric PAR for the inner portions of the Bay. In turn, this will influence the amount of submarine PAR available in the *Z. marina* zone. Further study is needed to determine the actual light requirements of *Z. marina* in an elevated sulfide environment, but this analysis suggests that light in conjunction with elevated sulfide levels could be limiting the current distribution of *Z. marina* in Thatcher Bay.

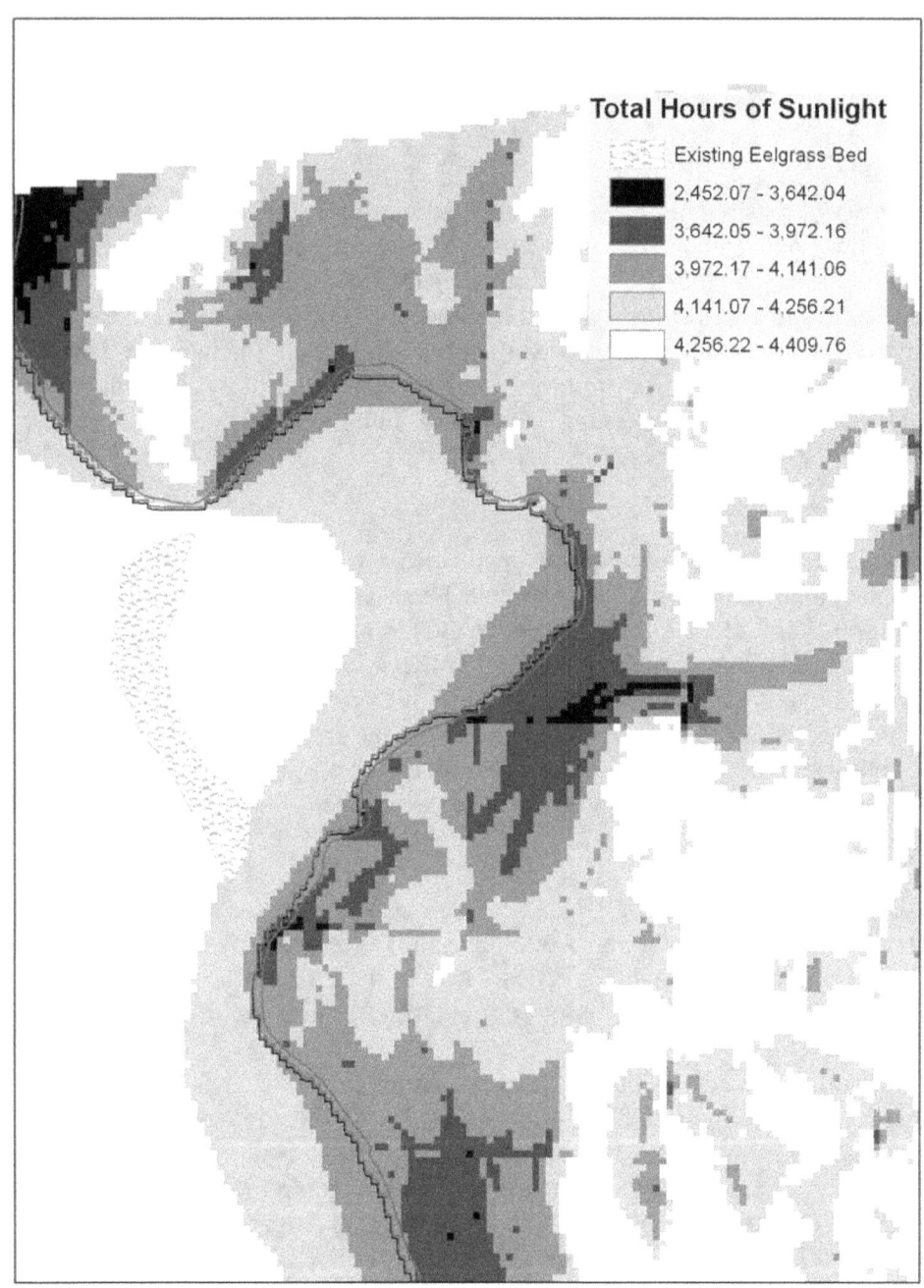

Figure 14. Map of total hours of direct sunlight for 2007 in Thatcher Bay and 2007 eelgrass cover (green stippling). Darker areas correspond to decreased total light availability.

Forage Fish Habitat

Forage fish are a vital part of the Pacific Northwest marine ecosystem. They feed directly on phytoplankton and other marine invertebrates, and in turn, provide food for birds, salmon, and other species. Maintaining healthy forage fish populations has been outlined as essential to the recovery of Puget Sound salmon populations by the Puget Sound Salmon Recovery plan (2007). Forage fish provide a trophic link between phytoplankton, invertebrates, and higher trophic levels, such as salmon. Forage fish is a general term, and in the Pacific Northwest, it refers primarily to three species of fish:

Pacific herring (*Clupea harengus pallasi*), surf smelt (*Hypomesus pretiosus*), and sand lance (*Ammodytes hexapterus*). This study focuses on surf smelt and sand lance, which are known to spawn in the upper intertidal zones comparable to those found in Thatcher Bay (Washington Department of Fish and Wildlife Fish Management Program 1997a, b).

Friends of the San Juans (FOSJ) conducted forage fish spawning habitat surveys in 2004; both Surf smelt and Sand lance were found to spawn on beaches in and around Thatcher Bay. Surf smelt spawning was documented in the areas adjacent to those covered by wood-waste in Thatcher Bay (Figure 15; Friends of the San Juans, 2004). Surf smelt and sand lance share similar spawning habitat requirements, although sand lance prefer sandy substrate (1 - 3mm), while surf smelt prefer sand to small gravel substrate (1 - 7mm; Washington Department of Fish and Wildlife Fish Management Program, 1997a, b). The nature of the fine wood-waste found in the southeastern corner of Thatcher Bay is not consistent with these spawning requirements.

Figure 15. Surf smelt spawning in Thatcher Bay, Washington, adjacent to the wood-waste impacted area (Friends of the San Juans, 2004).

Both surf smelt and sand lance require reburial of their egg masses by tidal action to a depth of 2-15 cm in order to develop (WDFW Fish Management Program, 1997a, b). At these depths, the anoxic conditions and elevated sulfide levels in the Thatcher Bay sediments would likely inhibit survival. There is a lack of data specifically highlighting the sulfide tolerances of surf smelt and sand lance. Based on research conducted on various life stages of marine and freshwater species we can draw several conclusions. First, egg masses are more sensitive than juveniles or adults to sulfide levels. Egg masses of freshwater and marine fish species begin to be impacted by sulfide levels at .014-.25 mg L^{-1} through increased mortality, malformation, and decreased development rates (Adelman and Smith, 1970; Office of Water Regulations and Standards, 1986). The sulfide levels in the first 6 cm of the Thatcher Bay sediments were 17.5 mg L^{-1}, several orders of magnitude higher than the minimum egg impacting levels. At [(this elevated sulfide level) 17.5 mg L^{-1}] any egg masses which may have been deposited would have a high likelihood of mortality.

The second conclusion is that, while juveniles and adults are much more tolerant to elevated sulfides than egg masses; they are still highly sensitive to elevated sulfide levels and exhibit avoidance behaviors at very low sulfide levels (Office of Water Regulations and Standards, 1986). Dissolved oxygen surveys suggest that the water column in Thatcher Bay is not anoxic in the summer months (Breems, unpub. data, 2007). This would allow for the oxidation of sulfide into sulfate within the oxygenated water column negating its harmful effects. Long-term monitoring of seasonal oxygen and sulfide levels in the water column is necessary in order to determine the effect elevated sulfide levels in the Thatcher Bay sediments has on local water quality. Reduced dissolved oxygen could impact the survival and habitat utilization of juvenile and adult forage fish, as well as migrating and resident juvenile and adult salmon populations.

Summary of Current Conditions

By using available historical data and field observations it is clear that past milling activities are responsible for the wood-waste present in the southeastern corner of Thatcher Bay. Coring and field operations in August 2007 confirm the presence of wood-waste in the intertidal/subtidal area of Thatcher Bay, and that it has persisted since the closing of the mill in 1942. The presence of wood-waste is most likely a result of the slow rate of decomposition in anoxic environments. Sediment sampling and analysis confirm that wood-waste presence has affected the composition of the sediment by increasing the organic content. Increased organic content leads to increased anaerobic bacterial activity, which creates a reducing environment with increased levels of sulfides that are toxic to several species of nearshore flora and fauna. The net effect is decreased density and diversity of the invertebrate communities and overall reduced habitat quality of the available nearshore habitat (Hyland and others, 2005).

The topography of Thatcher Bay in conjunction with elevated sulfide levels, which are influenced by the degraded sediment conditions, could contribute to a light-limited environment for *Z. marina* during the winter months. Under current conditions it is anticipated that *Z. marina* colonization would be limited. With improved sediment conditions there is potential for *Z. marina* colonization into certain portions of Thatcher Bay.

However, the greatest impact of the wood-waste presence in the intertidal areas of Thatcher Bay could be the reduction of potential forage fish spawning habitat. The elevated sulfide levels and sub optimal substrate as a result of the presence of wood-waste could also be limiting invertebrate presence and diversity in the sediment. The combination of reduced forage fish spawning habitat and reduced diversity of the benthic invertebrate community could reduce the value of Thatcher Bay for adult and juvenile salmon.

Thatcher Bay provides a timely and unique opportunity for restoration in the San Juan Archipelago. The combination of impaired nearshore habitat quality, and protected and intact backshore and upland areas, provides a strong rationale for restoration of Thatcher Bay.

Restoration Approaches and Alternatives

The goal of this project is to improve natural processes and habitat function of the nearshore habitat in Thatcher Bay by the remediation or removal of wood-waste in the southeastern corner of Thatcher Bay. The objective of this section is to identify the most feasible restoration strategy that meets the goals and objectives of this project. As such, generalized implementation plans are provided for each alternative. Restoration alternatives were ranked against criteria developed by the Thatcher Bay Project Team using a matrix. The Thatcher Bay Project Team used the matrix to guide the selection of a preferred restoration alternative. Following further discussion between Skagit Fisheries Enhancement Group (SFEG), Friday Harbor Laboratories, University of Washington (UW), and Washington Department of Fish and Wildlife (WDFW), the most feasible option(s) will be further developed and expanded to include permits, design, and preliminary budgets for the purpose of pursuing funding and implementation options. Appendix C provides a description of the ranking criteria and the results of the matrix ranking process.

Three general categories were considered (1) no action (2) capping the wood-waste zone with clean sediment, and (3) removal of the wood-waste. The Restoration Alternative Analysis section provides an overview of the results of the matrix-ranking process and the selection of a preferred alternative.

No Action Option

Due to the lack of recorded history, the conditions present in Thatcher Bay prior to Euro-American settlement are not known. Some fraction of the wood-waste which was deposited on the site 70-100 years ago is still present and the anoxic conditions result in a reduced decomposition rate extending the time required for natural recovery. The negative impacts of increased organic matter in the sediment matrix are well documented (Wang and Chapman, 1999; Koch 2001; Hyland and others, 2005). The reduced forage fish spawning habitat, impact to the invertebrate community, and degraded water quality will persist under the no action option. Thatcher Bay's protected status and relatively unimpacted backshore and watershed are starkly different than other areas in the region, increasing its current value as potential forage fish spawning habitat. Increasing forage fish spawning and forage habitat is timely considering current efforts to restore Puget Sound salmon populations as stated in the Puget Sound Chinook Recovery Plan (2007).

Sediment-Capping Option

The area adjacent to the project site in Thatcher Bay highlights the potential success of a sediment cap. This area experienced a blowout with the failure of the Spencer Lake dam in 1965. Based on historical photographs, it is likely that there was wood-waste present in this location prior to the failure of the dam. It can be hypothesized that the debris from the dam break either removed the wood-waste, transporting it into the active currents of Thatcher Pass, or capped it with the rocky upland sediments. In either scenario, it appears to have locally reduced the wood-waste impact as evidenced by the documentation of surf smelt spawning at the mouth of the creek (Friends of the San Juans, 2004).

Sediment capping is a mitigation or restoration strategy that is used frequently for contaminated marine sediments. The structure and effectiveness of marine sediment caps is debated in the literature (Thoma and others, 1993; Shull and Gallagher, 1998; Evison, 2003). Thatcher Bay presents a unique environment for a sediment cap, as the wood-waste is located within the intertidal zone.

Any sediment-capping solution would require the importation of appropriately sized cap material from an external source. The placement and size of the cap material would require additional survey and planning to account for the effects of tidal and wave energy over time on the site. The change in bathymetry of the bay as a result of the addition of sediment from a cap could require ongoing monitoring and maintenance to ensure its effectiveness.

Removal of Sediment Option

There is a wide array of methods available for the dredge removal of sediments (Phillips and others, 1985). The characteristics and conditions of Thatcher Bay are unique, such as the intertidal distribution of wood-waste and the shallow nature of the bay. This leads to two broad categories for sediment removal; land-based and water-based excavation of contaminated sediments. Both options involve importing appropriately sized substrate to replace excavated material, as well as the open-water unconfined disposal of contaminated sediments. The disposal method is contingent upon permit approval. Should open-water unconfined disposal be deemed not feasible through the permitting process, upland disposal to an appropriate facility will [could] be used.

The land-based removal would require the mobilization of excavation equipment via land or water, depending on the specific contractor. The excavation of the contaminated sediments would take place from the backshore above the project site. Removal of the intertidal sediments would be constrained by tidal movement and the ability of the equipment to be supported by the intertidal substrate. The use of a sheet pile dam may be required to increase the work window and allow access to the subtidal sediments.

There are many water-based dredge techniques. Final selection of a technique would be determined by the local availability and feasibility of use within the site. Preliminary investigations have revealed that mechanical and hydraulic techniques may be the most appropriate due to the water depth and volume of sediments to be removed. Mechanical methods would require the use of a crane or excavator equipped with a dredge or clamshell bucket. Sediment would then be deposited on a barge for transport to the open water disposal site. Hydraulic methods are similar, but would entail the use of hydraulic removal of sediments into a hopper or barge for transport to the disposal site. Both methods are feasible, but are contingent upon the local availability of equipment and operators.

Restoration Alternative Analysis

The analysis of the restoration alternatives via the matrix-ranking process allowed for the selection of a preferred alternative for restoration. The merits and feasibility of each alternative are discussed below.

The no action alternative was determined to be unsuitable to achieve the project objective of restoring habitat function to the nearshore areas of Thatcher Bay; this report has outlined the detrimental impact of wood-waste presence in Thatcher Bay. It was concluded by the project team that the "no action" alternative would not lead to the improvement of habitat quality for surf smelt, sand lance, and other nearshore-dependant species in Thatcher Bay. Therefore the project team rejected the no action option. Sediment-capping was also rejected by the project team because the intertidal nature of the site created a high level of uncertainty about the long-term effectiveness and stability of the sediment cap.

The project team ranked both the water- and land-based removal alternatives highly. Concern over the impact of a land-based removal operation on the intertidal and backshore areas, as well as, the ability of required equipment to operate on the unstable intertidal sediments, led to a lower ranking for the land-based method. Water-based removal was unanimously selected as the preferred alternative. It was concluded that a barge-based removal operation conducted over a short work window, would have the lowest negative impact and highest likelihood of success. The next phase of the restoration project is to use the findings of this report to complete the permitting process and finalize the removal design based on the selected alternative.

References

Adelman, I. R., and Smith, L.L., 1970, Effect of hydrogen sulfide on northern pike eggs and sac fry. Transactions of the American Fisheries Society p. 501-509.

Carruthers, T. J. B., Longstaff, B. J., Dennison, W.C, Abal E.G, and Aioi, Keiko, 2001, Measurement of light penetration in relation to seagrass Global seagrass research methods: Amsterdam, Short, F.T., and Coles, R.G., eds., Elsevier, p. 369-392.

Chemetrics. 2008. Analytical Method: Sulfide (total soluble). http://www.chemetrics.com/analytes/sulfide.html.

Dennison, William C., Robert J. Orth, Kenneth A. Moore, and others, 1993. Assessing Water Quality with Submersed Aquatic Vegetation. BioScience 43, no. 2 (February): 86-94.

Duncan, J.M. 1990. Measurement of Light Energy. In Seagrass research methods, ed. Ronald C. Phillips and C. Peter McRoy, 147-151. Monographs on oceanographic methodology, 9. Paris: Unesco.

Elliott, J. K., E. Spear, and S. Wyllie-Echeverria. 2006. Mats of Beggiatoa Bacteria Reveal that Organic Pollution from Lumber Mills Inhibits Growth of Zostera marina. Marine Ecology- An Evolutionary Perspective 27, no. 4 (December): 372-380.

Encyclopedia Britannica. 2008. Fetch. In Encyclopedia Britannica Online. http://www.search.eb.com/eb/article-9034138.

Evison, L. 2003. Contaminated Sediment at Superfund Sites: What We Know So Far. US Environmental Protection Agency, Office of Emergency and Remedial Response Workshop on Environmental Stability of Chemicals in Sediment. San Diego, CA, April.

Friends of the San Juans. 2004. Documented Surf smelt and Pacific Sand lance Spawning Beaches in San Juan County with a Summary of Protection and Restoration Priorities for Forage Fish Habitat. Final. Friday Harbor, WA: Friends of the San Juans. http://www.sanjuans.org/pdf_document/ForageFishFinalReport.pdf.

Gaeckle, J., P. Dowty, B. Reeves, and others, 2007. Puget Sound Submerged Vegetation Monitoring Project 2005 Monitoring Report. Washington Department of Natural Resources. Olympia, WA. www.dnr.wa.gov/Publications/aqr_nrsh_2005_svmp_report.pdf

Gayaldo, P. F. 2002. Eelgrass (Zostera Marina) Restoration Techniques. PhD dissertation, University of Washington.

Goodman, J. L., K. A. Moore, and W. C. Dennison. 1995. Photosynthetic Responses of Eelgrass (Zostera marina L.) to Light and Sediment Sulfide in a Shallow Barrier

Island Lagoon. Aquatic Botany 50, no. 1 (April): 37-47. doi:10.1016/0304-3770(94)00444-Q.

Hayner, N. S. 1929. Ecological Succession in the San Juan Islands. Chicago.

Holmer, M., M. S. Frederiksen, and H. Mollegaard. 2005. Sulfur accumulation in eelgrass (Zostera marina) and effect of sulfur on eelgrass growth. Aquatic Botany 81, no. 4 (April): 367-379.

Hubbert, L. 2007. Personal Communication. Personal Communication. June.

Hubbert, L. Letter. 2008. Blakely Island Forest Practices. June.

Hyland, J., L. Balthis, I. Karakassis, and others, 2005. Organic Carbon Content of Sediments as an Indicator of Stress in the Marine Benthos. Marine Ecology Progress Series 295: 91-103.

Koch, E. 2001. Beyond light: Physical, Geological, and Geochemical Parameters as Possible Submersed Aquatic Vegetation Habitat Requirements. Estuaries and Coasts 24, no. 1 (February 9): 1-17. doi:10.1007/BF02693942.

Mayhew, S. 2008. backshore : Oxford Reference Online. In A Dictionary of Geography. University of Washington: Oxford University press, May 27. http://www.oxfordreference.com/views/ENTRY.html?entry=t15.e245&srn=1&ssid=1150121104#FIRSTHIT, last accessed [date]

Nelson, D. W., and L. E. Sommers. 1994. Methods of Soil Analysis. In Methods of Soil Analysis, ed. D. L. Sparks, A. L. Page, P. A. Helmke, and others,, 1004-1005. 3rd ed. Soil Science Society of America book series 5. Madison, Wis: Soil Science Society of America.

Office of Water Regulations and Standards. 1986. Quality Criteria for Water. Environmental Protection Agency. http://www.epa.gov/waterscience/criteria/library/goldbook.pdf.

Pedersen, O., T. Binzer, and J. Borum. 2004. Sulphide Intrusion in Eelgrass (Zostera marina L.). Plant, Cell & Environment 27, no. 5 (May): 595-602. doi:10.1111/j.1365-3040.2004.01173.x.

Pentec Environmental, Inc. 1994. Biological Monitoring Report for Log Handling Operations in Thatcher Bay, Blakely Island. Edmunds, WA: Pentec Environmental, May 31.

Pentec Environmental, Inc. 1997. 1997 Wood Debris Monitoring Report for Log Handling Operation in Thatcher Bay, Blakely Island. Edmunds, WA, May 5.

Philips, R. C. 1984. Ecology of an Eelgrass Meadow in the Pacific Northwest: A Community Profile. FWS/OBS-84/24, Seattle Pacific Univ., WA (USA). School of Natural and Mathematical Sciences.

Phillips, K., J. Malek, and W. B. Hamner. 1985. Evaluation of Alternative Dredging Methods and Equipment, Disposal Methods and Sites, and Site Control and Treatment Practices for Contaminated Sediments. Prepared for Washington State Department of Ecology, by the US Army Corps of Engineers—Seattle District.

Project Restoration Committee. 2004. Focal Areas Assesment Report. Skagit Fisheries Enhancement Group.

Puget Sound Chinook Recovery Plan. http://www.nwr.noaa.gov/Salmon-Recovery-Planning/Recovery-Domains/Puget-Sound/PS-Chinook-Plan.cfm

Puget Sound Shared Strategy. 2005. San Juan County Salmon Recovery Plan.

Redman, S., D. Myers, D. Averill, and others, 2005. Regional Nearshore and Marine Aspects of Salmon Recovery in Puget Sound.

Roe, J. 2005. Blakely Island in Time. Montevista Press, December 15.

Shared Strategy Development Committee. 2007. Puget Sound Salmon Recovery Plan. Seattle, WA: Puget Sound Shared Strategy. www.sharedsalmonstrategy.org.

Shorelands and Environmental Assistance Program. 2002. Net Shore-Drift in Washington State. January 9. http://www.ecy.wa.gov/services/gis/data/data.htm#driftcell.

Short, F. T., and C. M. Duarte. 2001. Methods for the Measurement of Seagrass Growth and Production. In Global Seagrass Research Methods, ed. F. T. Short and R. G. Coles, 155-182. Amsterdam: Elsevier.

Short, F. T., and S. Wyllie-Echeverria. 1996. Natural and Human-Induced Disturbance of Seagrasses. Environmental Conservation 23, no. 1: 17-27.

Shull, D. H., and E. D. Gallagher. 1998. Predicting dredged-material cap thickness from data on benthic community structure. Site WEB: http://massbay.mit. edu/marinecenter/Publications/publication002/shull1998a.htm.

SPSS. SPSS 13.0 for Windows. SPSS Inc.

Suttles, W. P. 1951. Economic Life of the Coast Salish of Haro and Rosario Straits. College of Anthropology, University of Washington.

Thoma, Greg J., D. D. Reible, K. T. Valsaraj, and L. J. Thibodeaux. 1993. Efficiency of capping contaminated sediments in situ. 2. Mathematics of diffusion-adsorption in the capping layer. Environmental Science & Technology 27, no. 12 (November 1): 2412-2419.

Wang, F., and P. M. Chapman. 1999. Biological Implications of Sulfide in Sediment a Review Focusing on Sediment Toxicity. Environmental Toxicology and Chemistry 18, no. 11: 2526-2532.

Washington Department of Fish and Wildlife Fish Management Program. 1997a. WDFW -- WA State Forage Fish: Sand lance. http://wdfw.wa.gov/fish/forage/lance.htm.

Washington Department of Fish and Wildlife. 1997b. WDFW -- WA State Forage Fish: Surf smelt. http://wdfw.wa.gov/fish/forage/smelt.htm.

Zimmerman, R. C., J. L. Reguzzoni, S. Wyllie-Echeverria, M. Josselyn, and R. S. Alberte. 1991. Assessment of Environmental Suitability for Growth of Zostera marina L.(Eelgrass) in San Francisco Bay. Aquatic Botany AQBODS, 39, no. 3/4.

Appendices:

P — Penetration
R — Retrieval
Ss — Surface sediment
W — Wood-waste
S_W — Sediment/Wood
DS_W — Dense Sediment/Wood
BS — Basal Sediment

Appendix A. Coring Data Table: Raw data from sediment Coring August 2007.

Station	UTC	Lon	Lat	P	R	SS	W	S_W	DS_W	BS	Max_Depth_	Wood_Thick	total_dept	Comment
1	8/25/07 14:04	-122.81566	48.55243	0.41	0.41	0.14	0.27	0.00	0.00	0.00	0.41	0.27	0.41	NA
2	8/25/07 14:15	-122.81560	48.55230	0.33	0.20	0.00	0.20	0.00	0.00	0.00	0.20	0.20	0.20	Minimum wood-waste depth
3	8/25/07 14:35	-122.81562	48.55225	0.53	0.51	0.00	0.41	0.00	0.00	0.10	0.41	0.41	0.51	NA
4	8/25/07 15:10	-122.81538	48.55202	0.58	0.58	0.00	0.58	0.00	0.00	0.00	0.58	0.58	0.58	NA
5	8/25/07 15:35	-122.81559	48.55234	0.40	0.40	0.00	0.18	0.20	0.00	0.02	0.38	0.38	0.40	S/W comes before W see photo
6	8/25/07 16:04	-122.81577	48.55234	2.00	2.00	0.00	1.40	0.00	0.00	0.60	1.40	1.40	2.00	BS, clay shell hash 2cores
7	8/25/07 16:39	-122.81595	48.55228	0.72	0.44	0.05	0.31	0.00	0.00	0.10	0.36	0.31	0.46	NA
8	8/25/07 16:54	-122.81586	48.55216	1.89	1.53	0.20	1.03	0.00	0.00	0.31	1.23	1.03	1.54	2cores base fell out on first core.~12cm wood compaction
9	8/25/07 17:28	-122.81581	48.55202	1.07	0.82	0.11	0.19	0.40	0.00	0.12	0.70	0.59	0.82	~12cm wood compaction
10	8/25/07 17:47	-122.81572	48.55189	1.00	0.88	0.00	0.13	0.27	0.38	0.10	0.78	0.78	0.88	~12cm wood compaction
11	8/25/07 18:01	-122.81566	48.55176	1.05	0.82	0.03	0.17	0.14	0.00	0.48	0.34	0.31	0.82	NA
12	8/25/07 18:16	-122.81574	48.55157	1.15	1.00	0.00	0.00	0.46	0.35	0.19	0.81	0.81	1.00	NA
13	8/25/07 18:26	-122.81555	48.55164	0.60	0.60	0.16	0.29	0.15	0.00	0.00	0.60	0.44	0.60	Hit rock at bottom of core
14	8/25/07 18:37	-122.81548	48.55182	1.40	1.00	0.00	0.73	0.00	0.41	0.29	0.73	0.73	1.02	NA
15	8/25/07 18:43	-122.81554	48.55196	1.50	1.00	0.00	0.44	0.00	0.00	0.15	0.85	0.85	1.00	NA
16	8/25/07 18:50	-122.81563	48.55209	0.84	0.84	0.00	0.64	0.00	0.00	0.20	0.64	0.64	0.84	NA
17	8/25/07 18:57	-122.81568	48.55222	0.80	0.67	0.00	0.67	0.00	0.00	0.00	0.67	0.67	0.67	.67 is a minimum wood depth
18	8/25/07 19:09	-122.81553	48.55228	0.42	0.39	0.00	0.39	0.00	0.00	0.00	0.39	0.39	0.39	.39 is a minimum wood-waste depth
19	8/26/07 16:44	-122.81613	48.55221	1.05	0.98	0.00	0.29	0.00	0.00	0.69	0.29	0.29	0.98	NA
20	8/26/07 16:56	-122.81604	48.55209	1.05	0.88	0.05	0.25	0.00	0.00	0.58	0.30	0.25	0.88	NA
21	8/26/07 17:05	-122.81599	48.55196	1.10	1.05	0.00	0.28	0.00	0.00	0.77	1.05	1.05	1.05	At least 10cm compaction
22	8/26/07 17:22	-122.81617	48.55189	1.10	1.05	0.00	0.00	0.00	0.20	0.85	0.20	0.20	1.05	Wood-waste very sparse
23	8/26/07 17:30	-122.81587	48.55176	1.10	1.05	0.07	0.08	0.00	0.23	0.67	0.38	0.31	1.05	NA
24	8/26/07 17:46	-122.81584	48.55169	1.10	1.05	0.07	0.15	0.00	0.17	0.66	0.39	0.32	1.05	BS, softer clay
	8/26/07 17:57	-122.81592	48.55151	1.10	0.89	0.00	0.06	0.00	0.26	0.57	0.32	0.32	0.89	NA
26	8/26/07 18:33	-122.81537	48.55170	0.65	0.50	0.00	0.50	0.00	0.00	0.00	0.50	0.50	0.50	compaction 10cm, lost top 5cm
27	8/26/07 18:38	-122.81538	48.55186	0.87	0.80	0.00	0.80	0.00	0.00	0.00	0.80	0.80	0.80	NA
28	8/26/07 18:56	-122.81541	48.55201	0.59	0.46	0.00	0.46	0.00	0.00	0.00	0.46	0.46	0.46	NA
29	8/26/07 19:03	-122.81548	48.55214	0.55	0.48	0.00	0.48	0.00	0.00	0.00	0.48	0.48	0.48	NA
30	8/26/07 19:10	-122.81559	48.55241	0.65	0.57	0.00	0.57	0.00	0.00	0.00	0.57	0.57	0.57	NA
31	8/26/07 19:15	-122.81570	48.55252	0.52	0.42	0.00	0.42	0.00	0.00	0.00	0.42	0.42	0.42	NA
32	8/26/07 19:20	-122.81588	48.55246	0.85	0.62	0.00	0.57	0.05	0.00	0.00	0.62	0.62	0.62	S/W comes before W

Appendix B. H2S Toxicity Thresholds. Adapted from (Wang and Chapman 1999) to include species likely to be found in the San Juan Islands.

Species	$\sum[S(-II)]^a$ (mg L^{-1})	pH	Endpoint[b]
Amphipod *Rhepoxynius*	1.47	8	48-h LOEC
	1.6	8	48-h LC50
Amphipod *Eohaustorius*	1.92	8	48-h LOEC
	3.32	8	48-h LC50
Amphipod *Anisogammarus*	0.2	8.2	96-h LC50
	3.2	8.2	24-h LC50
Amphipod *Corophium*	1.4	8.3	24-h LC50
Amphipod *Gnorimosphaeroma*	5.2	8	96-h LC50
Urchin *Strongylocentrotus*	0.1	8	48-h NEOC
	0.13	8	48-h LCEC
	0.19	8	48-H EC50
Urchin *Lytechinus*	>.1	8	49-d mortality occurred
	>10^c	8	49-d mortality occurred
Shrimp *Crangon*	0.64	8	1-h LT50
Crab *Cancer,* zoeae	0.5	8.1	96-h LT50
Crab *Cancer,* first instar	1	8.1	96-h LT50
Mussel *Mytilus*, embryo	0.05	8	48-h NEOC
	0.09	8	48-h LOEC
	0.1	8	48-H EC50
Mussel Mytilus	1.9	8	96-h EC50
	>50	8	96-h LC50
Clam *Macoma*	6	8.2	96-h LC50
Oyster *Crassostrea*	1.4	8.2	96-h LC50
Polychaete *Nereis*	5.76	8	24-d LT50
Polychaete Nereis	4.8	8	96-h NOEC
Polychaete *Capitella*	>16	8	3-h LOEC in settlement time

[a] Concentration expressed as total sulfide ($\sum[S(-II)]=[H_2S]+[HS^-]$). At Ph 8, $[H_2S]\sim0.09\sum[S(-II)]$.

[b] EC50 = concentration that causes 50% sublethal effect; LC50 = lowest-observed-effect concentration; LT50 = exposure time that causes 50% mortality; NOEC = no observed effect concentration.

[c] Pore-water total sulfide concentration in the presence of sediment

Appendix C. Thatcher Bay Nearshore Assessment Restoration Matrix.

Project objective: Improve natural processes and habitat function of the nearshore habitat in Thatcher Bay by the remediation or removal of wood-waste in the southeast corner of Thatcher Bay

The initial phase of the Thatcher Bay project was to assess the current conditions of Thatcher Bay. The assessment provided a description of the distribution and impacts of wood-waste in Thatcher Bay. The second phase of this project is to develop a preferred restoration alternative based on the findings of the report. To achieve this, a restoration matrix was developed to evaluate the four restoration alternatives. Ranking criteria were: Ecological services, socio-political and likelihood of success.

The objective of the project is to restore the habitat function to Thatcher Bay. Cost is an important consideration in any restoration activity, but does not serve as an effective primary ranking criterion when attempting to determine the best alternative to improve habitat function. For this reason cost is a non scoring criterion. Cost becomes an important selection criterion in the process of selecting the preferred alternative between two alternatives which similarly achieve the stated objective. Therefore cost is incorporated into the matrix as a ranked criteria meant to guide the final selection of a preferred alternative.

Ranking Criteria:

Ecological Services
a) Spawning habitat
There are many different species of vertebrates and invertebrates that could spawn or reproduce on the restored substrate. This project is focusing specifically on potential improvement to Surf smelt and Sand lance spawning substrate.

b) Benthic flora and fauna
The restoration alternative will positively impact multiple species of the benthic invertebrate community and sediment dependant flora.

c) Species diversity
The restoration alternative will contribute to improved species diversity and use by various trophic levels in Thatcher Bay.

Socio-Political
a) Local Landowners
Landowners of the impacted area are willing to participate in the restoration alternative.

b) State/Federal resource managers
The restoration alternative meets the guidelines of state and federal agencies.

c) PSP regional objectives
The restoration alternative aligns with the stated objectives of the Puget Sound Partnership.

d) Precedence
The restoration alternative sets a precedent for similar sites in the region

Likelihood of Success
The restoration alternative meets the objective of the Thatcher Bay project.

Cost of Restoration alternative
List the expected implementation costs and rank the projects from lowest to highest cost (1-4).

	No Action	Sediment Capping	Water based excavation	Land based excavation
Function/ Ecological Services a) **Spawning habitat** b) **Benthic fauna and flora** c) **Biodiversity**	a) b) c)	a) b) c)	a) b) c)	a) b) c)
Socio-Political a) **Local landowners** b) **State and Federal resource managers** c) **PSP regional objectives** d) **Precedence**	a) b) c) d)	a) b) c) d)	a) b) c) d)	a) b) c) d)
Likelihood of Success Will alternative achieve objective	a)	a)	a)	a)
Cost of restoration alternative • List potential costs • Rank in order of expected cost (low to high)				

Master List: compilation of all rankings provided by the 5 reviewers.

	No Action	Sediment Capping	Water Based Excavation	Land Based Excavation
Function/Ecological Services				
a) Spawning Habitat	-5	3	5	4
b) Benthic fauna and flora	-5	-1	5	5
c) Biodiversity	-5	2	5	5
Socio-Political				
a) Local Landowners	-2	0	4	0
b) State and Federal resource managers	-3	-2	5	1
c) PSP Regional Objectives	-5	2	5	4
d) Precedence	-5	0	3	4
Likelihood of Success				
Will alternative achieve objective	-5	-2	4	2
Total	-35	2	36	25

32

Reviewer	No Action					Sediment Capping					Water Based Excavation					Land Based Excavation				
	1	2	3	4	5	1	2	3	4	5	1	2	3	4	5	1	2	3	4	5
Function/Ecological Services																				
a) Spawning Habitat	-	-	-	-	-	+	+	-	+	+	+	+	+	+	+	+	+	+	+	+
b) Benthic fauna and flora	-	-	-	-	-	+	0	-	-	0	+	+	+	+	+	+	+	+	+	+
c) Biodiversity	-	-	-	-	-	+	+	+	-	0	+	+	+	+	+	+	+	+	+	+
Socio-Political																				
a) Local Landowners	-	0	0	0	-	0	0	-	0	0	+	0	+	+	+	+	-	0	+	-
b) State and Federal resource managers	-	-	0	-	-	0	-	+	-	-	+	+	+	+	+	+	+	-	+	-
c) PSP Regional Objectives	-	-	-	-	-	0	0	+	+	0	+	+	+	+	+	+	+	+	+	0
d) Precedence	-	-	-	-	-	0	0	0	-	+	+	0	+	+	0	+	+	+	+	0
Likelihood of Success																				
Will alternative achieve objective	-	-	-	-	-	0	0	-	-	0	+	0	+	+	+	0	-	+	+	+
Total	-8	-7	-6	-6	-8	3	1	0	-3	1	8	5	8	8	7	7	4	5	8	2

1) Robert Warinner, Watershed Steward, Washington Department of Fish and Wildlife
2) Perry Welch, Project Manager, Skagit Fisheries Enhancement Group
3) Alison Studley, Executive Director, Skagit Fisheries Enhancement Group
4) Joel Breems, Graduate Student, University of Washington Botanic Gardens
5) Sandy Wyllie-Echeverria, Research Faculty, University of Washington BotanicGardens

33